INTERPLAY

A Collection of poems by

Brenda V. Ackroyd

Don Bosco Publications

Don Bosco Publications
Thornleigh House, Sharples Park, Bolton BL1 6PQ
United Kingdom

ISBN 978-1-916546-19-6
©Don Bosco Publications 2024
©Brenda V. Ackroyd

The moral rights of the author have been asserted.

All rights reserved. No part of this publication may be reproduced, stored in a retrieval system or transmitted in any form or by any means without the prior permission in writing of Don Bosco Publications. Enquiries concerning reproduction and requests for permissions should be sent to The Manager, Don Bosco Publications, at the address above.

Front cover illustration Robert Clark/Unsplash

Printed in the UK by Jump DP

Contents

Introduction v
A convert's first prayer 9
Choosing faith 11
Jesus of Nazareth 13
Third person 14
Alpha and omega 16
Two hopes 18
The open window 19
For prisoners, freedom 21
Intersect 24
Hyacinth trinity 25
Spring thoughts 27
Summer thoughts 29
Autumn thoughts 30
Winter thoughts 32
A year of trees 33
Forest fire 34
Living water 35
Hidden treasure 37
Mirror lake 38
Night and day 39
The Advent wreath 41
On the way to Bethlehem 42
Joseph 43
The first Christmas 44
Cana miracle 45
The hour 46
Last Supper 47
The Garden of Gethsemane 48

In the Upper Room	49
The seed	50
Manchester Cathedral	51
Picture of an old lady	52
Human nature	53
In the window	54
Knitting	55
Curtains	56
Time	57
The tale of a fearsome preacher	59
Silent parables	61
Saint John the Baptist	62
The prodigal	63
Demolition	64
Elements of contrast	65
Nothing ventured…	66
The writer and the book	68
Covid	72
In time and space	74
A rosary in verse	75

Introduction

This collection of poetry has accreted slowly over a period of more than thirty years. I am not one of life's naturally prolific poets; but something happened in my life which triggered a spate of creativity. This produced a number of poems, and happily continued down the years, albeit more intermittently, enabling me to write the later verses in this book.

In the late 1980s I began a return into the Christian faith. In 1990, I became a full member of the Catholic Church. It changed my life profoundly. It has continued to change me ever since.

God had hovered in the background of my childhood, in my Baptist parents and my Methodist Sunday School. I heard the stories and drew the pictures, but God was never really discussed at home. In my early teens, Girl Guiding introduced me to church parades in the local Anglican church. This church, with its high pillars, stained-glass windows and beautiful words, struck me as deeper than the rest of life. I chose to be baptised and confirmed there at the age of fifteen.

I was quite devout for a few years, and loved many things about Jesus and his Church, but as university approached, I decided the hard-headed realism of the age was the truth. There was no kingdom of heaven, no eternal justice. It was a kind of escapism—even wish-fulfilment. I felt I had reached maturity at last, facing up to the grim reality that the world was simply ours to live in, ours to try to make a little better, if we could.

This philosophy served me well for years. I worked as an English teacher, married my husband John, brought up our two children, tried my hand at writing, and served for some years as a local councillor—all without a faith in God.

I never felt the need to reconsider. In fact, when unexpected circumstances led to my working closely for a period of time with a deeply committed Catholic colleague, I wondered if his faith had ever been challenged, if perhaps my attitudes might disillusion him.

How wrong I was! I owe him a huge debt of gratitude for patiently talking about faith with me. I could not help but see how real God was to him. I could not help but notice a special quality of peace and balance in him, which I had not met before. It made me wonder whether my decision had been wrong. It made me see the beauty of belief in one greater than oneself. It brought recognition that there really was a spiritual element in our human nature, which I had been denying. No wonder then that, although I had hardly admitted it, there had been moments in my life when things lacked meaning. There had been times when I was not sure where the different roles of wife, mother, teacher and other things centred.

This good friend became my sponsor three years later when, after a great deal of reading and reflecting and visiting of churches and finally a Rite of Christian Initiation of Adults, (RCIA) course, I entered the Catholic Church.

The first poems in this collection are the ones I wrote during the beginning of my journey back to God. They reflect both the tentativeness of my initial explorations of the spiritual, and the effort to come to understand the teaching of the Church. I was a mature woman now; I felt I had to make a real effort to grapple with and investigate in depth the ideas I was considering accepting as the truth. What a dawning of wonder, though, came with my conversion. Not just immediately, but ever after. There is no end to the discoveries God reveals to us. Hence the poetry-writing continued.

Most of these poems are about faith and aspects of our journey with God. Some of the later ones, though, are not religious. Some came about because I belong to a writers' group, and this led to occasional experimentation with different forms of poetry. I am one of those people who like doing puzzles, so complex and restricted poetic forms have sometimes presented an irresistible challenge. Whether the results are a success, you may judge!

After the first few poems, they are not in order of composition. I have tried to arrange them in such a way as to provide both continuity and variety. I have tried to include groups of the secular verses between the ones which reflect more directly on holy things. The latter are certainly in the majority, because God became and remains central in my life. It is in the spiritual that my life coheres. It is in the interweaving of our humanity and God's divinity that life catches fire.

For this reason, I took the title of this book from a poem addressed to the Holy Spirit:

> *"He" is the least of titles you have won,*
> *Sword of God's wisdom, river of His love,*
> *Fire of His truth; and still the same today,*
> *For us, you weave the leaping **interplay***
> *Between God's life and ours.*

A convert's first prayer

Forgive, Lord,
My frail daring
To approach.

One step
At once
Is all that I can…
Hardly that
Having nothing quite
Articulate
To speak,
Child in new worlds
As I am.

Gravity disinvented
Might loosen things
To something like
The dislocated landmarks of
My life.
Old certainties are
Insecured,
Untrustable,
Like lights
Winking through rain-spots
On a wind-blown pane.

Rescue now
Lies in a different
Discovering.
Not in the mental
Following of complex tracks
Laid arduously
In the past works of men,

But in the full self's
Helpless
Trustful
Reaching across dark
Without a hold
On strands of known
Experience.
A leaning into space
And being prepared to fall;
A giving at full risk
Of death or pain;
A self-revealing
Beyond shame.

So that the thing
I used to think I was
Is not.
Or is not here
In these eternal spaces
Faith must cross;
Is not to Him
To whom I am
Unfinished vulnerability,
A child unborn,
A need to be remade,
A frailty
Self-aware
Which yet aspires
To dare
To love God
And has hopes
Of meeting
Him
In prayer.

Choosing faith

Not like a dawning, pleasing realisation
As the last piece of rational argument
Falls into place and proves the case complete.
Nor like an overwhelming strength which masters
Me and holds me in emotional thrall.
There is no proof and no compulsion here.
Simply, the choice is mine. But not like
"Shall we stay in the States, or go back home?"
No calculating of the pros and cons,
Or counting lists of points, answers the call.
Nor trusting intuition on its own:
"Well, this feels right; I'm happier this way."
Hunches are not a trusty way to truth.
So it is not so simple after all.

For it is all these things and more. Of course
Within the mind ideas and arguments
Re-form and scatter like kaleidoscopes,
While in the heart flares a response of love
To chants and gentle statues and good words
Long-lost regretfully those years ago
When I shut church doors, turned my back, and faced
What I then thought was truth; that God did not
Exist; our world was ours alone to make
Or mar, to live in till death ended time.
Is it just growing old weakens resolve
And makes me turn for rescue from life's lack
Of centring and lack of depth to faith,
As our sad young ones to their crack or crime?

It came from seeing someone kneel in church,
The thought, like fresh air in a fetid room,
That there is such a thing as holiness,

That there is grace in goodness greater far
Than man alone can gain. That man is not
Complete till he admits his incompleteness.
That was the seed from which I think it grew,
In secret firstly, rooting in the soil
Of my grave need and fed by all the beauty
Of God's glorious world. Slowly the strange
Otherness of the church, my not belonging,
Lurched into grief which carved the way for wonder
As all God's words and mysteries, spurned so long,
Took life, and grew in strength and depth and range.

It was a double birth; two worlds perceived –
My stunted self and God's immensity –
Whose mutual awareness was my hope.
Not because it brought ease or an escape
From problems which could now be left to God,
For that's not so: more that I craved to be
Allowed to face its dangers, meet demands,
To journey somehow back across the wastes
Of Christless years, to waken in myself
The denied soul, the disused channels, break
An opening for God's love and mine to flow,
So that I might grope through my cavern's dark,
Knowing the rocks were there for feet to hold,
Yet having to feel for them, trust, and not mistake.

Jesus of Nazareth

God trod this earth once, day by day,
And felt the sand between his toes,
And smelt the fish and the sea-breeze,
And heard the sound that hammering makes
On the clear air, and saw the eyes
Of those who loved him, and of those
      Who quietly watched, awaiting his mistakes.

How fine his breathing must have felt
Through nostrils into lungs divine.
How brightly sunshine must have poured
Its light into his dazzled eyes.
How sweetly evening's shadows must
Have cooled the senses of the one
      Who was both fully man and all our Lord.

How great his anguish, realising,
In all man's heartless greed and pride,
Aggression, hate and selfishness,
His Father's grief. How strange that tears
Ran helplessly from his cupped face
Into the gentle palms of hands
      Which could heal others' suffering and fears.

How deep his love, to seek no rest
From sorrowing his Father's loss.
How infinitely good his choice
To disregard sweet joys of earth
And for our sins to pay the cost
In agonies which seared frail sense
      To forge our road to God upon the cross.

Third person

I understood you as a spirit of peace,
A wondrous, hazy presence of our God,
Deep, big as daylight.
So when they first referred to you as "he"
It jolted things.
Not just for gender reasons, though
I couldn't think of you as male or female
Since, before time had ticked or space outstretched,
Before man or woman lived,
You were.

When God in timelessness brought forth his Son,
The moment they were separate
You existed: their entwinedness,
The bond between them, love. You made the third.
One triangle, one God, one family
Forged in the patient-burning will of God
To make new worlds and fill them up with life.
Yet you were undefined, a kind of language, almost.
Not a person, surely. Not a "he"?

But you voiced truths into the minds
Of early prophets; you dropped like a sea-diving bird
Into our world to concentrate the whole divinity
Of God into the tiny scope of the new seed
You placed within a virgin's womb.
And when grown into manhood, on the brink
Of Jordan baptism and deeper trial, it was to you
Christ owed the over-hovering, imbuing all his human life
With the light breaking from the love-urged heart
Of his almighty Father, heaven-pent.
And when, after his death, you flamed
Over the heads of those gathered to wait,

They changed, new-powered.
"He" is the least of titles you have won,
Sword of God's wisdom, river of his love,
Fire of his truth; and still the same today,
For us, you weave the leaping interplay
Between God's life and ours. Your breath ignites
The wick within our waxen selves
And in its candle-flame we touch your heights.

Alpha and omega

I kneel before you and beneath you
Yet within your love, almighty Father,
Origin of all—of space and time, our planet earth,
Life, laughter, tragedy, beauty and loss,
All that we know and what lies still unseen.
Words cannot compass you, my God, so these
Poor strands of language only serve to glance
At facets of your Godhead, show perhaps
How far we may explore you, though to you
Our insight's plunge may seem the paddling of youth
On shallow verges of the ocean of your truth.

And sometimes, Father, those dramatic coasts,
Where we confront you, may shelve suddenly,
Or break in jagged rocks, or frighten us into retreat
From cliffs or caves where the sea's muscles
Pound against our foothold land and shattered spray
Mimics our vulnerability before your might.
For while it's easy, Lord, to give you praise for
Lovely things—for children's voices, for warm fires,
For sunlight edging cloud, and smells of rain—
There are times too, we come to you in pain.

You cannot, Lord, be blind to those who grieve,
Bereft of a sweet child before its time. You surely know
How fiercely agonies of war grasp hearts, and tear up
Whole communities. You feel the prisoner's fear.
How, Father, could your loving plans allow
The fires that split volcanoes, spill and scorch our earth?
Cureless, infecting viruses? The mud that slides
And stops the mouths of dwellers on our mountainsides?

You foresaw all. You knew some spirit-lives
Would yearn for independence, turn to pride
And greed and violence. You knew their strife
Would be enacted through our lives. You wanted that
And not some doting love of puppet-toys for the
Indulgence of their master. You let go our strings.
So rock-sure is your love, you gave us grounds
To choose you or reject you, left us free to find
Our own self's journey through life's crags and calms,
Loving us all, watching for broken souls, grown bold
Enough to mine their utter depths and find your gold.

Two hopes

"Well, we can hope," I hear one say.
Another shakes his head.
"I've brought my brolly—just in case
We get the rain instead."

What is this creature, hope, to them—
Inconstant, like a dream?
Capriciousness that comes and goes
A fluctuating stream?

It seems their disappointment waits,
An actor in the wings.
Hope's a mere puppet on their stage
With frayed and fragile strings.

God's children know a different hope,
A virtue and a power,
Dependable and trustworthy
In every single hour.

This hope is not a fickle stream,
It's built on mountain rock
That stands throughout eternity:
God's passion for his flock.

The open window

You hardly see the filaments of wings.
Frantic speed blurs them as they lift and lift
The weighted tiny body up the glass.
Drawn, resolute, plain furious perhaps,
The insect butts its head against the pane
In frenzied concentration of desire
To reach the other side. Above, the transom
Window gapes. Does it not smell the air?

Wings wilt; the body sinks down to the sill.
But only briefly. Then its task resumes.
Consumed in effort, yet it seems to float
Lazily up like smoke, and upward still
Until, encountering the solid frame,
It drops back down the window to the view
Of trees and skies that seem to promise flight,
Yet trap him in a glassy prison cell.

Maybe we scorn his tiny insect mind
Or maybe, with a paper, help his climb
Over the window frame and into space—
And joy, we would imagine. For we too
Have to escape sometimes. We feel the need
To break out of the humdrum of our lives,
To rise above the squabbles, talk and lies,
And with full-stretched wings lift into the skies.

For mostly we too bump against the glass
Of disappointment when our dreams disperse,
Frustration when our plans disintegrate,
Or disillusionment when nothing lasts.
Yet we could find the opening, breathe the air
Of a sweet world of beauty, truth and grace,

20

If we would only dare to trust in faith
To show us pathways logic cannot trace.

For prisoners, freedom

"Shades of the prison-house," the poet explained,
"begin to close upon the growing boy."
As if, once childhood's wakening is past,
We become trapped within our life's confines,
Imprisoned in the cage of our own
Space and time.
But is it true?

Surely we retain our powers to choose?
Think of all the small selections,
What to wear and what to say,
That occupy us every day.
And then the bigger things:
Which job? Which way?
Which woman for my wife?
Which man? Choosing is life.
Is it a prison, then,
Whose confines have to span
The inexhaustibility of choosing man?

Is it a prison when
Its walls are not of stone
Blocking the sight of persons unbeheld,
But are instead the fragile edges of perception,
Touching the unknown
Which we can contemplate
And try to reach
Into…?

Perhaps not with the sharp immediacy of sense,
Nor with the sound analysis of intellect,
But in that gentle depth
Where sense, emotion, thought

All meet with something
Light as breathing
Which transforms,
Like alchemy,
And lifts and opens us,
Because its mystery touches into life
An inner core of mystery in ourselves
And brings us to the biggest choice of all.

Do we decide
That these
Intimations of a world outside
Our space and time dimensions
Just delude us into letting slide
Our hold of what is real?
Can we find truth
By staying thus confined
Within the limits of the human mind?

Or do we rather make
The leap
To faith in a reality which far transcends
Bodily sense or intellectual grasp,
But is explorable by those
With open minds and unproud hearts
Whose spirits dare to ask
For God
To shape their lives?

Once we have yearned
To love
The one who crafted this blue gem of earth,
Set it on perfect track and gave us life
To walk upon its lands and watch its skies,
Then we begin to see with wiser eyes
How God's love moves all things.
His glory blazes beauty everywhere,
His truth explains, His power explodes

The puny computations of our
Stumbling thought,
Just as His gift, our saving through His Son,
Broke through time's membrane,
Wrote the Word in flesh,
Confined the infinite,
Made weakness strength, death life,
And helped us see
That Christ indeed sets all the prisoners
Free.

Intersect

White bird,
Sky bird,
Bright as holiness,
Captured my gaze.
Gull in December,
Flashing its catch of sun,
Stretching blade wings,
Slicing long, angled lines,
Taut as wires, high
Above the city's winter streets.
Tunnels of shadow these,
where my car crawled,
While I rose heavenward,
Fastened to the geometry you traced,
Straight-winged,
Solitary
Aerobat.

As you so cleanly etched,
Like skates on ice,
Those arcs and lines of flight
On cobalt sky,
The beauty of creation
We were sharing
Carved diagonals of love
Across my heart,
And burned that moment
On eternity.

Hyacinth trinity

Beyond eyesight
The Father lives
Hidden from us, as a flower bulb
Lies invisible in damp, dark earth
Yet breathes in secret,
Driven to root and swell,
Perhaps by the creative power
That is the core of God,
To break out of itself its living flower.

Right from the centre thrusts
Its sturdy tip of leaves
Safely encasing all its folded future
Pushing it to birth
As God the Father once begot the Son
To build new worlds from love and yet remain
Confined with him in their eternal land
Until, when springtime came,
He newly broke the crust of this our ground
And opened his display to human sight.
So came God's Son to earth
To flower in mortal flesh and bone;
Strong, tender, lovely, petal-bright.

Hyacinths cast their perfume
On the air we breathe,
So that our senses bloom at the invading
Glory of their fragrance.
Our loneliness may flare too into warmth,
Because the reckless blossoming of God,
The spilling of Christ's blood,
Bequeathed his Holy Spirit to us all.
A richer legacy than flowers' breath,

Which dies the instant petals crisp and fade;
For when Christ's paled flesh crumpled on the cross
Evil was disempowered,
New life was free,
The Spirit came for all
And death brought no more loss.

Spring thoughts

The green lace lift and fall
Of springtime boughs
Easter You to us.
Trees break our eyes into new realms of green
As you our lives into salvation.

Leaves finger out to us,
Unfold, uncurl, stretching
Their taut new skin against the air.
Green fronds heal over winter's scars,
Refreshing landscape's vast renewing womb.
Hedges grow fat between the cropless fields;
Showering lime trees break
The city's lines,
And every beech and plane, each oak and elm
Prints its distinctive shape upon the sky
To re-horizon us.

The fragile leaf has power to change our world.
It builds the forest's architecture new,
Gentles the pelt of rain,
Absorbs the midday sunshine's heated blaze
And dapples it for us to walk beneath
In shifting underseas of glints and pools
Of tranquil green and haze.

All the sweet weight
Of foliage of spring, suspended
Above ground on branch and stem,
Resting in total trust upon the air
Like faith, is God's grace-gift fresh-seen.

Leaves re-enact the rising of our Lord,
Breaking to new life after winter's worst,
Wielding a strength, like His, which is not built
On forceful conquest
But defenceless love,
Whose beauty nurtures us, heals us, forgives,
Wombs us through mortal life upon this earth
Into our spring of heavenly rebirth.

Summer thoughts

Summer's like being stranded inland,
Ageing in silence in a breezeless heat
Far from the fresh, wild, sea-edge cries of gulls.
Spring's memories have dwindled
Into nonexistence
Like unheard sounds of sea on distant shores.

Thus new things root in us,
And reach and range, filling our space
Until, too close to strike us, being known so well,
They grow unknown, and imperceptibly
Their powers fade.

So poets lose youth's naked touch of words,
Bare contact, like with hands against the skin,
Yet choose to tussle still with language on the page.

And so we wander from our trust in God
Into a wilderness of doubts and fears,
Yet struggle still to come to Him in prayer.

For not all fades, familiarises, dies.
Lightning can still bring deluge from the skies.
God's Holy Spirit breathes, and re-ignites our lives.

Autumn thoughts

Leaf fall, the flare of fires,
Lengthening darkness and the mornings slow
To stir low-lying mist and let the sun
Soften the early-frosted grass blades on the lawn.

Life learns to hibernate in burrows,
Tubers, seeds, by firesides,
Settling to wait long, dormant days and weeks,
Until new sun's warmth pulses sap through veins.

We try to think of death as a transition,
A crossing-over journey here to there.
But where? Where there's no return?
No spring re-planting? Where?
Some other where than this our cycling earth
Whose suns and snows prompt growing and decay.

Eternity. It pales imagination,
Strands us in helpless groping
Through venerated words and eyes and dreams,
Towards a few fragmented shafts of truth
Of an elusive, endless world of light
Where choirs blend unworldly harmonies
And white robes flutter in a breeze
From angels' wings.

How short imagination falls.
I dare to think that heaven is no such place.
Light, yes—for light's God grace that helps us see
And heaven is seeing all. And angels, yes, perhaps,
But not just chanting in some floaty haze.
Here and there, past and future, may be lost,
But that means all God's truth at once perceived,

All life's variety, deepened by love,
Seen inside out perhaps, soul before skin.
So Christ saw, when he stood upon our shores,
And so will we when we are one with Him.

Winter thoughts

Winters are warmer now
With some blue days between
The damp and drear of black tree skeletons
Brooding over autumn's leavings
Mulched now underfoot.

The magic snows of childhood come no more,
Unless to haunt the memory
With gentled contours of the school-walk landscape
And that held-breath of silence
Snowfall always brought,
Like distilled wonder.

Perhaps the muffling of every sound
In that new white-upholstered world,
Or the stark black and whiteness of the scene,
Snow-blossomed trees and crispness in the air
Combined into a fragile purity
We treasured while it lasted,
For it lacked defence against
The harsh incursions
Of scraping spades on driveways,
Tyre-tracks, footprints, thaw.

Or was it that in some dim way
It gave us a foretasting of God's mystery.
It showed us how Christ's loving mercy,
In gentle silence falling,
Obliterates the ugliness of sin,
Washes our world,
Reveals the breathless wonder
Of our truest home.

A year of trees

The silhouettes of January trees
Stand starkly outlined on wide, shifting skies.
In February's frost bare twigs may freeze

Till March sunlight persuades the sap to rise.
This plumps the buds in April, so that May
Blossoms with frills of flowers to bless our eyes.

The whites and pinks of cherries hold their sway
Before laburnums loose their golden chains
And foliage thickens till the branches weigh

Heavy, and cast deep shade across the lanes
Of summer months, as June and July pass
With fulsome trees that shelter us from rains.

August wearies them and the whole mass
Of leaves grows dusty. Yet September's seeds
Are ripening fast within them, and the grass

Beneath receives the windfalls—and this feeds
October's hungry birds even as leaves fall
And cold winds pile them up amongst the weeds.

November's rains pelt from their cloudy pall
And mulch the leaves as food for next year's roots.
December may perhaps cast her snow-shawl

Over the landscape till trees wear white suits,
And children tramp beneath their boughs in boots.

Forest fire

Sequoia Sempervirens, redwoods tall,
Spend their Sierra winters deep in snow;
But summers bring them heat, and in its glow
Forests catch fire and damage spreads its pall.
How is it that these flames, which warm our hall
And bake our bread and make our senses flow,
Spread terror on the wind, an awesome foe,
Leaving no place unscathed, consuming all?

A fiery colour glows in redwood bark,
But it grows thickly-textured to protect
The veins of sap beneath it from fire's claws,
So that, though flames may leave their fatal mark,
Sequoia trees revive and stand elect
To plant their saplings on cleared forest floors.

Living water

Fragile the mist
Drifting a blessing over Pennine moors
Blurring the bones, chilling the flesh of hills,
Pearling sheep's wool,
Like dew-fall fresh on spiders'
Filigree.

Stronger the silver spikes
Slanting from iron clouds in autumn storms,
Dimpling canals and ponds,
Darkening walls, drumming like conscience
On the panes of windows,
Canopies and roofs,
Till water sluices over roads and spreads in fields,
And river currents muscle into
Power.

Implacable the might
Of frozen glaciers' relentless crawl
Through massive mountain strongholds,
Whose granite spines
Icy teeth slice through,
Creating giant grooves
Of naked valleys,
Grinding the fractured boulders
Slowly into
Sand.

Welcome the wet
To thirsting roots and wasted limbs
In dehydrated lands
Where the first liquid fingers
Trickle along dry, stony watercourses

Carrying dust grains, like columns of ants,
Before they swell in spate
To burst the seeds and break trees into leaf,
Re-greening landscape, answering prayers,
Rivering lifeblood into folds and fibres,
Opening each capillary to its
Salvation.

Hidden treasure

In children's books it is the glint of gold,
The coins and jewels, in an aged chest,
Brass-bound and hidden in a gloomy cave.
In ancient sagas too, the secret hoard
Of golden vessels in the monster's lair
Provides what glory-seeking heroes crave.

In everyday, though, have we quenched the thirst
To seek out precious secrets? Have we lost
The thrilling quests that left us all aghast?
Maybe, but we have hidden treasures still,
And these are not just legends and old dreams
Spun by the minds and pens of writers past.

These things are real; they touch us every day.
They light our senses as we pass their way:
The perfume that lies hidden in the flower,
The chime that breaks from silent clocks each hour,
Spring leaves held secretly in winter trees,
Still water's sudden rippling in the breeze.

A violin lies mute within its case,
But let the player's bow run on its strings
And glorious music is released. It sings.
The lifeless chrysalis, when time is right,
Cracks so the butterfly escapes its bonds
And warms its wings in readiness for flight.

A child's real treasure does not lie in books.
It lies within them, growing, yet still furled.
Who knows what this small boy may one day be,
Or if this little girl will change the world?
For, once revealed, their talents might inspire,
Might spark deep change and set the world on fire!

Mirror lake

Stark against feather-clouded cobalt skies,
The rugged lines of ancient Lakeland fells,
Sentinels, guard the wooded slopes and vales
Where grey stone cottages lie hid from eyes.

Aslant the green field, dipping, tilting lower,
A solitary curlew takes its flight,
Where sedges shift and flicker in the light
Along the lake rim's horizontal shore.

Along the lake rim's horizontal shore,
Where sedges shift and flicker in the light,
A solitary curlew takes its flight
Aslant the green field, dipping, tilting lower.

Where grey stone cottages lie hid from eyes,
Sentinels guard the wooded slopes and vales,
The rugged lines of ancient Lakeland fells
Stark against feather-clouded cobalt skies.

Night and day

Fading rays of sunlight flame the undersides of cloud,
A glorious fanfare in the sky before the daylight fades
Leaving a sky of indigo with piercing stars endowed,
While air cools and forests fill with night's deepening shades.

A glorious fanfare in the sky before the daylight fades,
The sunset closes down the day and ushers in the night
While air cools and forests fill with night's deepening shades,
And damp falls on fronds where prey eludes the night owl's flight.

The sunset closes down the day and ushers in the night;
Windows darken, noises fade, most human life seeks sleep,
While damp falls on fronds where prey eludes the night owl's flight,
And moonlight casts its pallid glow, and silvers oceans deep.

Windows darken, noises fade, most human life seeks sleep,
While on its axis through long hours, our planet slowly spins,
And moonlight casts its pallid glow, and silvers oceans deep,
Until eastward a new light grows and a fresh dawn begins.

Still on its axis through long hours, our planet slowly spins,
And shadows roll, tides turn, night creatures scuttle on their way,
Because eastward a new light grows and a fresh dawn begins,
And birdsong and fingers of light rouse us to greet the day.

The shadows roll, tides turn, night creatures scuttle on their way,
Till sunlight rounds upon us, bringing colour on the hills,
And birdsong and fingers of light rouse us to greet the day,
Waking us to activity and all life's joys and ills.

The sunlight rounds upon us, bringing colour on the hills,
Sharpening landscape's contours, chasing shadows from the towns,
Waking us to activity and all life's joys and ills,
As people bustle, traffic moves, late trains are met with frowns.

Sharpening landscape's contours, chasing shadows from the towns,
The sun, unless it's lost in cloud, we see pursue its track,
As people bustle, traffic moves, late trains are met with frowns,
Until the work-day's over and home comforts call us back.

The sun, unless it's lost in cloud, we see pursue its track,
As hours slide by, tasks are complete, the children finish school,
Until the workday's over and home comforts call us back
Into familiar rooms, where love and caring are the rule.

As hours slide by, tasks are complete, the children finish school,
The day moves towards evening, and the sun dips in the west.
Within familiar rooms, where love and caring are the rule,
Lamps are lit up, while some set forth and others take their rest.

The day moves towards evening, and the sun dips in the west,
Till fading rays of sunlight flame the undersides of cloud.
Lamps are lit up, while some set forth and others take their rest
Beneath a sky of indigo with piercing stars endowed.

The Advent wreath

A small child lights the candles every week,
One more each time until four Advent lights
Flicker to life and make the ring complete.
The candle in the centre all these nights
Waits, as we do ourselves, for Christmas Day,
Waxen and chill until a hand ignites
The wick, and something new comes into play.

The yellow flame extends and reaches high;
An inner peachy glow transforms the wax.
No longer cold, it radiates. And I
See in it both how mortal man reacts
And how the birth of Jesus changes things.
Without him we stay cold; our nature lacks
The glow of inner peace and love's bold wings.

Once lit by him, we cast a gleam around,
Lighting our world and making shadows dance.
We spread his fragrance, speak without a sound,
And burn our wax in service, in the trance
Of blazing in the Spirit, reaching higher,
Until, as Jesus died to bring our chance,
We, like all candles, melt into his fire.

On the way to Bethlehem

Imagine endless miles of road,
The rhythmic grind against her bones,
The womb-weight bumping with the donkey's lurch,
The figure, weary, wilting, half-asleep,
Of this girl-woman, almost at her time.

Her body drained, but maybe in her heart
Joy leaps, abruptly breaking from the hold
Of steady and well-measured expectation,
Like laughter at a funeral,
A lightning bolt out of the mind of God.

Joseph must think she is too tired for thought,
Or that she struggles between trust and fear.
He lifts an arm around her to console;
She turns such bead-bright smiling eyes to him:
"A Son of God!" He's silenced by her words.

Then he leans closer as they echo still.
And there it blossoms on this treeless road:
The flower of hope, the presager of joy.
He sees she has no fear, no nerves astir,
For she is given to God and He to her.

Joseph

It was a cave, a home for beasts—no more.
The midwife who attended was a stranger,
Kneeling amid the rushes on the floor
To birth a child destined to live with danger.

My pacing in the darkness failed to ease
The doubts which deep within began to bud.
Why me? Why us? What strange events were these,
That I should father one not of my blood?

I tilted back my head to see the sky,
Where pin-sharp stars lay spread across the night.
Things stilled. I felt God's presence. Who was I
To doubt your gift, Lord, of this child of light?

A single star gleamed more than all the others
Just as a new cry broke. I rushed within
To greet my girl-bride, now the queen of mothers,
Who bent to kiss her newborn boy, God's kin.

The first Christmas

It wasn't like our tinsel Christmas trees,
Or dishes piled with turkey or mince pies,
Or Christmas songs from Kings broadcast to please
The churchgoers amongst our family ties.

From God's eternal heart the need to ease
The torment of the devil's enterprise,
In twisting men from grace, planting disease,
Provoked an act of love wider than skies.

From vast eternity to earth there came
The Holy Spirit to a village girl,
Bearing the tiny seed of hope to earth.
She nurtured it in quiet, made no claim
To greatness, like an oyster with its pearl,
Until she brought the Son of God to birth.

Cana miracle

Who can lay hands on love? It has no shape.
It bubbles up like water from a well.
Sometimes it floods and spreads a level cape
Across our fields, then sinks and goes to dwell

In secret places, while our lands grow dry.
Yet while some passions fade, others endure.
Who will explain to us, who'll tell us why
One man is rich in love, another poor?

Is it that, like the wine at Cana's feast,
Our love exhausts itself, supplies run out?
Can we not from our limits be released
So that our human love may know no drought?

Through God's grace, yes, and power of love divine,
Our feeble feelings change to full red wine.

The hour

My hour has not yet come, he said,
When Mary pointed out
The wedding feast was short of wine.
Did Jesus suffer doubt?

At any rate he filled the jars
With wine of the best sort,
Obedient to his mother's prompt,
Creating it from nought.

It was the first of many signs
Prefiguring his power,
And mirroring that pouring out
Of self at his true hour.

Before that came, he taught us all,
Forgave, and healed and showed
Our greatest wealth in heaven lies
And love to all is owed.

And when his hour came at last,
He heard his Father's call,
And gave his life upon a cross
Dying to save us all.

Last Supper

Christ's hands held
And blessed the bread.
His fingers tore;
Felt the crust break;
Freed its warm fragrance;
Offered it to all.

Other hands seized him;
Split the flesh with nails;
Released his glory
For God to offer all.

So now the hands
Of priests are his.
His fingers break
The host before our eyes.

He hands himself to us;
The broken grain
Sunk in the darkened earth
To rise again
And grow afresh in us.

We are the hands
Of his new body
Here on earth.
Spirit-equipped
To feed and serve
The world.

The Garden of Gethsemane

'It will not die.'
Our guide explains
The olive's attributes.
Hack at its branches how you may
It still puts forth new shoots.

These trees can live
Two thousand years.
Their gnarled shapes testify.
Christ's eyes could have been turned to them
That night he chose to die.

'Gethsemane'
Means olive-press.
The fruits are squeezed for oil.
And this was where our Lord was crushed;
His blood fell on this soil.

But like the tree
That springs anew
Our Saviour was not felled.
He rose into New Life more rare
Than ever man beheld.

Our guide moves on
Leaving behind
Bent trunks and sinewed limbs.
Yet we look back and for Christ's pain
Give thanks in silent hymns.

In the Upper Room

They gathered in the Upper Room
Quietly praying until—BOOM!
All heaven broke loose, the building shook,
They gazed around and one said, "Look!"
Above their heads there swirled a flame.
It danced upon them like a game
Until from faulty men they changed
By God's huge power re-arranged.

The seed

Our Lord made very clear indeed
The grain of wheat must fall and break.
Unless it dies it stays a seed;
Once cracked, new life from it will wake.

The grain of wheat must fall and break
And sink into the dark, deep earth.
Once cracked, new life from it will wake,
Shoots, stems and grains will come to birth.

And sinking in the dark, deep earth,
The seed is lost; its life seems done;
Yet shoots and grains will come to birth
And from them bread for everyone.

The seed is lost; its life seems done,
As did our Lord's upon the cross;
But from there bread for everyone
Comes from his sacrifice, his loss.

As did our Lord upon the cross,
We too must share his earthly strife
Since from his sacrifice, his loss,
We gained forgiveness, love, new life.

We too must share his earthly strife,
Dying to self is just the start;
To gain forgiveness, love, new life
We must let him transform our heart.

Dying to self is just the start.
Our Lord made very clear indeed
We must let him transform our heart;
Unless it dies, it stays a seed.

Manchester Cathedral

If you could watch it as a fast-speed film
Run backwards, you would see its rising tower
And hunkered spread of stone holding its ground
While round it whirling traffic dwindles, buildings fall
And rise to lowlier heights, until just small brown houses
Squat by the lanes the faithful walk to church.

Then if you went inside, reversed the film, you'd see
The tides of changing people filling and refilling
The pillared chambers of this old stone heart.
A slow and steady pulse of seeking, finding, leaving,
Circling, returning, as bees to a hive,
To that still central place where we can taste
The honey of God's love. Where hums
The spinning top of hectic city life about
The steady axis of this rock of faith.

Picture of an old lady

Her son supports her slow walk down the street
Towards the country inn on faltering feet.
White-haired, in summer shoes, his arm in hers,
She's like my mother in her final years.
And how she would have liked this rustic scene,
This village, its old cottages, its green.

She'd look at flowers across the owner's fence,
Relishing colours, shapes and summer scents.
She loved the gentle pace of rural ways;
Trips to the country were her favourite days.
Houses and gardens, walks by streams or lakes,
Ending in tea rooms with mouth-watering cakes!

In younger days, of course, she liked the noise
Of hectic family life, of girls and boys
Shrieking round house and garden, in some game,
Or softer, more harmonious sounds that came
When her hands touched the old piano's keys
And Schumann's music spread its moody ease.

In Cornwall once I took her to "Trerice":
A lovely house, her kind of paradise,
Its grey walls sunlit and its flowers unfurled
To gift their fragrance freely to the world.
I never will forget her thankfulness
As she said she felt "drunk with happiness."

Human nature

What a machine the human body is:
An engine which breathes air and exhales waste,
A food system and ceaseless pump for blood.
If this was all God made, we'd think it graced.

Yet minds enrich our human lives still more,
And senses bring the gifts that kindle love;
Through eyes we grasp the outlines of the hills,
The marshland edge, the sun's flash from above.

The sounds of talk and laughter, hymns and songs,
Inspire us, while hands touching bring to birth,
Like the fresh feel of air, or fire's warmth,
Emotions, yearnings, seekings after worth.

So, far from cold machines, our depths are stirred
To find the roots of beauty, truth, God's Word.

In the window

That's Violet—she sits in the window and stares,
Her bony hands knotted and textured with veins.
Sometimes she must think there is no one who cares,
As her mind takes to wandering its own twisted lanes.

Her bony hands knotted and textured with veins—
They once stitched and knitted and cooked for us all.
Though her mind takes to wandering its own twisted lanes,
It was sharp as a pin once, a match for each call.

They once stitched and knitted and cooked for us all,
Those hands, when the war stopped and let life re-form.
It was sharp as a pin and a match for each call,
That mind of a WAAF in her stiff uniform.

Those hands, when the war stopped and let life re-form,
Were a wife's and a mother's—my grandma's quite soon—
And that mind of a WAAF in her stiff uniform,
Though trained on the radar and in the ops room,

Was a wife's and a mother's—my grandma's quite soon—
Giving love to each one of us, full and unstinting,
Though trained on the radar and in the ops room
To spot destinations at just the first hinting.

Giving love to each one of us, full and unstinting,
She'd no thought for herself, as she learnt in her training,
To spot destinations at just the first hinting.
So it hurts now she needs us, and sharpness is waning.

She's no thought for herself, as she learnt in her training.
That's Violet—she sits in the window and stares,
And it hurts now she needs us, and sharpness is waning.
Sometimes she must think there is no one who cares.

Knitting

A humble craft, the knitter's, yet it joins
The fleece from sheep, the colours from the dye,
With fingers' deft work, faster than the eye,
Creating something worth far more than coins:
A handmade gift, that forges links between
The maker and the wearer: mother, child;
The soldier at the front, out in the wild,
With women gathered, knitting khaki green.

If wool threads catch and break, snagged on a nail,
The work unravels—yet could be re-used
For blankets, shipped to those by crisis bruised.
In our own lives sharp snags may us impale,
Pull threads, dismantle friendships—yet forgiving
May knit us back to wholeness, heal our living.

Curtains

We draw our blinds against cold winter's dark,
Cherishing homely comfort
Round our fire-lit hearth,
Warming ourselves
Like children curled in beds,
Safe within pastel-pictured walls.

Curtains complete our barricades,
Excluding what does not belong
And what's unknown.

Yet ignorance of what may hide
Within, behind, beyond an opaque screen
Creates suspense we simply love to break.
We yearn to tweak the fabric's edge,
To peep into the moonlit night,
Raise up that theatre curtain to expose
The drama's lighted world.

When glowing morning opens curtains
On God's sunlit land,
It floods our hearts.
Is it because our spirits can foresee
The glory of that final day
When earth itself will split apart
Disclosing to our startled eyes
God's homeland,
Our eternal destiny?

Time

Time is the regular tick-tock-tick,
Remorseless progress of hands on a dial,
Marking the pace of the daily routine,
The commute, the commitments,
The outings and meetings,
The pulse of your diary,
The tolling of bells and the chiming of clocks.

Time is a tyrant, enforcing attendance,
Rushing us onward to catch that train.
Time blows the whistle
To line up the children
Or finish the cup tie
And settle the score.
Time erects walls that the eye cannot see.

Time also burdens and clogs us and hinders,
Dragging his feet when the bus fails to come,
When hope fades for the news
We've expected for ages,
When sleep hovers close
But always eludes us,
Time is a prison without any bars.

Time is a fabric that stretches and gathers,
Pulled by differing threads in our lives.
It races or lingers
It crawls, or it clots
Completely in shock
Like the blood in a vein
When accidents happen and stop all the clocks.

While minutes tick by with monotonous rhythm
God watches all from a place so beyond
All the clutches of time,
That within them and through them
Time's count is discounted
And God holds it all,
Like a marble that turns in the palm of His hand.

The tale of a fearsome preacher

(*with apologies to Hilaire Belloc*)

When he was born, they named him Saul.
He seemed to have no faults at all.
He grew up strong, he grew up fine,
In Jewish rites he toed the line,
And was instructed long and well
In the school of Gamaliel.

As he matured, he gathered clout.
He knew the law inside and out,
And when the fans of Jesus spread
And leaders really wished them dead,
He saw the problem's one solution
And launched his trade of persecution.

When Stephen's angel-face was stoned,
Praise and approval he intoned.
He spied on Christians everywhere
And loved to drag them from their lair.
He spared not one, arresting all,
Chaining them to their prison wall.

When our Lord's fans by Saul were found
Much glory did to him redound
And so his reputation grew
And those who feared him not were few.
But all unknown, his changing fate
Around the corner lay in wait.

Though he who works against the Lord
Mere humans might cheer and applaud,
God's plans are of a different kind.

He blazed his truth in Saul's dark mind,
And Paul a whole new life began,
Transformed into Christ's greatest fan.

Till, after years of wondrous preaching,
All corners of the nations reaching
With the gospel of God's love,
Justice and mercy from above
Cast Paul in chains, curtailed his leisure,
But filled him with the Spirit's treasure.

Happy who learns this truth to live:
What you receive is what you give.

Silent parables

You often spoke to men in tales,
Stories of shepherds, trees, or vines,
Till your disciples learned at last
To read between the lines.

We tread upon an earth that speaks
To those who still their hearts to hear
The silent parables of one
Whose kingdom hovers near.

The washing river over stones,
The sand rinsed daily on the beach
Show how your mercy purifies,
Takes sins far out of reach.

Stout tree trunks stand against the gale
Like faith in times of strife or doubt,
Although the seasons change, leaves fall,
And all shifts round about.

When new leaves break from buds in spring,
As dawn sun lights the edge of cloud,
The new life, the fresh hope you bring
Almost speaks out aloud.

When shining light is fractured, into
Colours arched across the sky,
Each seems distinct, like all the folk
Your love alone can unify.

Saint John the Baptist

(*who unusually has two Feast Days: of his birth on June 24 and of his death on August 29*)

The herald of the Lord, the Baptist, John,
Who preached repentance in the wilderness,
Knew he'd give way to a far greater One,
The Lamb of God, whose love was measureless.

Yet Jesus called John greatest of his kind
And, certainly, tales of his birth ran wild:
His mother far too old; husband assigned
To silence for his doubts about the child.

Yet John lived bravely, voicing what was right
About the woman Herod made his wife.
It brought John prison chains and worse one night
When women's schemes and butchery took his life.

Small wonder John's accorded two Saints' Days;
His birth and life and death all merit praise.

The prodigal

As if it surfaces into the light
Out of the autumn shades of Rembrandt's work,
The old man's face exudes relief,
His tremulous, protective, thankful love
At his lost son's return, exhausted, home.

But see the grooves of grieving on his brow,
The shadowed cheek, the weary-watching eyes.
His joy's not surfaced yet into flamboyant
Festive geniality; it goes too deep.

This is a father harrowed by the hurt
Of carefree youth's contemptuous dare,
Whose strong love yet carved gift out of himself
Of half of all his family possessed,
To free the boy to suffer his own fall,
And keep alight the slender flame of hope
Which clung within the wounded Father's heart.

A hope that after headstrong failure,
In a new darkness, like a fractured seed,
This son might put out tendrils of new life.

A hope he's nurtured daily in his prayer,
Watching the road, with love, to see
And welcome that returning boy
Whom now at last, today, a moment since,
His eyes beheld, and now his hands
Can hold, so that the broken bond
Of filial love, like ours with God,
After the disobedience of years,
Mends in humility and heals in tears.

Demolition

New space shocks now, where once, framed by these trees,
Its bulk stood firm: our ark, our church, broad-roofed
Like a brown nesting bird, wings spread over her brood.

The roof is smashed, the tower felled and spread
In ugly piles of bricks like innards spilled
Across the smooth-tiled floors where once we knelt to pray.

Here once the incense smoked, and candles flamed,
The water splashed and wedding music played.
Our lives interconnected and God changed us all.

It's more than bricks and beams they tackle here,
These yellow raiding monsters, angle-armed,
Tipping their spoil of wreckage into battered skips—

As if the whole could be carted away.
But there are things here no machine can touch:
Memories held like jewels on the strings of time.

Words our priest spoke which sank deep in our hearts,
Times we rejoiced, or wept, or glimpsed the power
Of all God's mystery, or knew the Spirit's fire.

As fine as gossamer, this filigree
Of past relationships, of turning points,
Of times our daily lives mingled with the divine.

Yet, indestructible, it hangs and stays
Not only in this space and in our hearts,
But etched outside of time in God's eternal mind.

Elements of contrast

Out of God's loving mind springs all creation:
Land, sea and air, fire, waterfalls and trees:
Gifts which bring blessings, yet cause consternation.

From earth grow flowers beyond imagination,
Rain fosters crops, quenches our thirst with ease.
Out of God's loving mind springs all creation.

Yet earth's tectonic plates cause fragmentation
And waters swell to drown and flood the leas.
Gifts which bring blessings, yet cause consternation.

The family fireside counters tribulation.
Good smells of hay or hops ride on the breeze.
Out of God's loving mind springs all creation.

Yet flames can tower in cruel conflagration
And hurricanes whirl round to smash and seize.
Gifts which bring blessings, yet cause consternation.

Faith is the only way to God's salvation;
Trusting his plan encompasses all these.
Out of God's loving mind springs all creation,
Gifts which bring blessings, yet cause consternation.

Nothing ventured...

A girl jumps from a wall
Into her father's arms.

A yachtsman circumnavigates the oceans
Of the world
Alone.

What trust!

What joy lights in the father's eyes,
Catching her weight against him,
Clutching the warmth of his own child's
Belief.

What triumph—
When the sailor's prow points home,
When all the water's worst is overcome
And his home harbour nears,
Its grey quays clustered with regrouping friends
Who've come to cheer, to celebrate
The glory
As his journey ends.

Each child of God
Makes leaps.

Each one with faith
Must leave His world behind
To dwindle in the shrinking wake of distance
And set forth through the seas of years
Without a tiller, save
The power of the Holy Spirit in His sails.

God's arms can catch us all.
Joy lights His eyes.

And when our lifelong voyage nears its close,
Can you not see Him waiting on the quay,
Ready to share with us
His victory?

The writer and the book

There lived a man who dreamt all day
Of a wonderful new world.
All night its stories came to him;
Its children round him swirled.

Its life became too big for him
To hold within his head.
He set his pen to paper, writing
Down these lives instead.

His fingers ran away with him,
As he set the scene with glee:
Blue seas and mountains, fields of green,
Where his people would be free.

Both young and old began to set
Their roots down in this land.
They raised up families there and made
A living as each planned.

And as they ploughed, and built their homes,
And harvested the earth,
Their fears were few, their children grew;
His world had come to birth.

He loved to make the seasons turn,
To see their harvest joy,
The homely fires of wintertime,
Spring love in girl and boy.

He watched their interweaving lives,
Conflicting now and then,
But when blood fell upon the snow,
He had to halt his pen.

This had not stained the dream he'd had.
Who brought about this strife?
As his swift pen rushed on again,
The darkness spread through life.

As each scarred chapter ended and
He broached a fresh new page,
He hoped they'd learn from past events
And not succumb to rage.

But arguments grew into wars,
And many fought for power,
So that they lived in luxury
While others learnt to cower.

How could he teach that everyone
Was valued in his world,
And that, if they could live in love,
True joy could be unfurled?

It meant a change in all his plans,
Otherwise life was doomed.
The more he pondered what to do,
The more new visions bloomed.

He could not bluntly change their lives
And make them full of love.
He liked their independent ways
Not forced by one above.

But he could bring into their midst
A new man, just like them,
But gifted with the wisdom of
The one who held the pen.

He planned an obscure birth for him,
A healing life of prayer,
In hopes that of their own free will
They'd choose new ways to care.

And many people changed their lives
And served their fellow men.
They came to love the silent source
Of all that came to them.

Unfortunately many more
Ignored his wise advice,
Still in the thrall of jealousy,
Or greed, or murderous vice.

The writer's dream moved on apace.
A deeper world came clear;
It seemed that he had always known
This paradise so dear.

It was to be a perfect land
Where evil could not tread,
Where those who trusted in his voice
Would follow as he led.

Alas for all the tainted folk!
Something must wash them clean,
Naught but the willing blood of one
He sent could seal this dream.

This wondrous man agreed to die
To set all people free
Of sickness which had seized on them
And brought such pain to be.

How our good writer now rejoiced
To see his perfect realm
Thrown open to humanity
Whom nought could overwhelm!

He let the book run on and on.
It never was to end.
The death of one saved all the souls
That ever he had penned.

The first world went on, stained with harm,
As from the times now past,
But those who sought the man who died
Found glorious love at last.

Covid

You put the brakes on, Lord.
You stopped us in our tracks.

All the pell-mell forward motion,
Working, selling, gaining, winning,
Climbing, rushing, buying, spending.

You put the brakes on, Lord.
We almost heard their squeal,
And shook as carriage after carriage
Jolted down the line.

Disrupting all the exploitation,
Digging, mining, burning, spoiling,
Using, dumping, felling, wasting.

You put the brakes on, Lord.
You stopped us in our tracks.

All those theories of expansion,
Earning, spending, flying, meeting,
Building, gaining, driving, wrecking.

You put the brakes on, Lord.
We looked out
Through windows.

Was it the first time we saw?
The trees massacred?
The oceans poisoned?
The islands flooded?
The forests burned?

You put the brakes on, Lord.
You stopped us in our tracks.

We saw the cracks in heating earth
And crops rotting in rain.
We saw people driven from homes
Clinging to boats at sea.
We saw the destitute on streets
And those who didn't care.

No wonder, Lord,
When the virus came,
You let it stop us
In our tracks.

Will we just re-start the engine?
Or, disoriented, will we,
Dazed by the experience,
Open all the carriage doors,
Climb out and look
With new eyes on your earth?

You put the brakes on, Lord.
You stopped us in our tracks.

Help us change direction, Lord.
To give our children futures.

Turning, changing, weeping, learning,
Saving, sharing, mending, planting,
Giving, loving, tending, caring.

You put the brakes on, Lord.
You stopped us in our tracks.

In time and space

On this fair planet, poised in time and space,
Kept at the perfect distance from the sun,
We owe huge thanks to God's creative grace.

For seas and fields and hills are held in place,
The clouds drop moisture and the rivers run,
On this fair planet, poised in time and space.

Because the seasons one another chase,
Bringing us winter's dark and summer's fun,
We owe huge thanks to God's creative grace.

For, though we cannot set eyes on his face,
He sent, to live amongst us, his dear son,
On this fair planet, poised in time and space.

He knew this gem of earth, this special place,
And since he saw our ways would profit none,
We owe huge thanks to God's creative grace.

He took our flaws and ills in his embrace,
And by his death a triumph for us won.
On this fair planet, poised in time and space,
We owe huge thanks to God's creative grace.

A rosary in verse

No thunderbolt portended God's great breakthrough to the earth;
A gentle angel asked a girl to bring a son to birth.
No adulation met her "Yes". She travelled lonely ways;
Then joy as mothers met and unborn infants prompted praise.
No palace housed his birthing, just a stable in the night,
And yet the angels' singing and the star revealed heaven's light.
They brought him to the temple with a love that went so deep
They heard the words of Simeon and knew at times they'd weep.
Flashes of fear came early, for no rosy path they trod;
They lost him, searched, then found him talking of his Father, God.

When, grown to manhood, humbly he sought John to be baptised,
God's words of love and mighty Spirit split apart the skies;
And at his mother's prompt, a striking miracle gave sign
Of all the changed new life he'd bring, when water turned to wine.
Three years he wandered, teaching truth, offering sinners grace,
Healing the sick, rebuking pride, giving to love first place.
Many were drawn to follow, but three only saw revealed
The blaze of glorious light in him which normal life concealed.
He was the Christ, they knew, and though he spoke of death's dark pall,
He promised food from flesh divine to sanctify them all.

Night gathered in the garden as he faced his fears and prayed
For strength to do his Father's will, to choose to be betrayed
To capture, and to falling victim of men's vengeful urges
Bearing the wicked onslaught of their barbed and ugly scourges.
They pierced his head with mocking thorns, yet he knew sharper pain
In heartfelt grief for those for whom this death would be in vain.
On bruised and bloodied shoulders they let fall the cross's weight;
He took it for his destined course, all sins to expiate.
And when they nailed and lifted him upon that shameful wood
They crucified the Lord of life, the source of all things good.

Although all hopes died there, as he was laid within a tomb,
Death could not hold him, and instead Christ broke our sinners' doom.
He rose up to his Father in the heaven from which he came,
Taking our human life there, so we'd never be the same
Because it opened up a way God's spirit could inspire
Each one of us, when he came down on heads like tongues of fire.
Mary was with them, praying, always faithful to her son,
So, when her days were ended she was lifted to the one
Who crowned her Queen of heaven, first of all the saints above,
A wondrous path to Jesus, drawing us into his love.